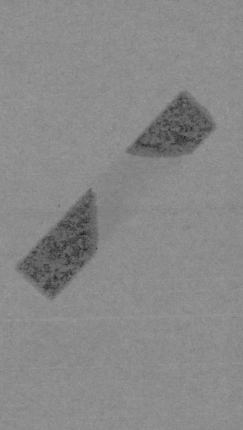

THE MINIATURE
FLOWER ARRANGEMENT
BOOK

FRONTISPIECE

MIXED SPRING GARDEN FLOWERS   Spring/April

Container :   Bronze incense burner. Height 3 ins. (76·20 mm.).
Contents :   Chaenomeles japonica.
                 Muscari.
                 Narcissus, 'Cheerfulness'.
                 Forget-me-not.
                 Anemone.
                 Polyanthus.
                 Auricula.
                 Rosemary.
Description : This bronze incense burner is one of a pair. The lid contains a
                 small hole under the figure of a lion, through which the scented
                 smoke would rise. It is of Japanese manufacture and is about eighty-
                 five years old. Wire netting is used as a support for the material,
                 and, although the container is a mere 3 ins. in height, it holds
                 sufficient water for the needs of this delightful collection of spring
                 flowers. The treatment of the colours in this small group, as with
                 all arrangements of mixed flowers, is to arrange the colours in
                 groups of twos and threes in order to emphasise that particular
                 colour.

C12   flower arrangement $4

flower arrangement

MARGARET AND GODFREY BEST

THE MINIATURE
FLOWER ARRANGEMENT
BOOK

CHARLES SCRIBNER'S SONS. New York

A-7-71 (1)

Printed in Great Britain

Library of Congress Catalog Card Number
SBN 684-12442-4

CONTENTS

to our son
Martyn
and our nieces
Ann, Elizabeth,
Alexandra,
Catherine Douglas
and
Catherine Scott

ACKNOWLEDGMENTS

Many years ago I had the idea of making a collection of seasonal miniature flower arrangements; this was heartily endorsed by Constance Spry and so for her encouragement and enthusiasm I have reason to be very grateful.

For some years I was a regular contributor of articles to the *Gardeners Chronicle*, therefore our thanks are due to Mr. Colin Parnell, the Editor, for allowing us to use our photographs and articles originally published in the *Gardeners Chronicle*.

To Mr. H. H. Muirhead, Executive Director of the British Colour Council, with whose permission I quote from the first set of the Horticultural Colour Chart produced by the late founder director, Robert F. Wilson.

Sir Sacheverell Sitwell who kindly grants me permission to quote from the chapter 'The Old Primrose and Polyanthus' from his book *Old Fashioned Flowers* published by Country Life.

To Mr. John L. Cassidy who has taken such care with the colour processing.

To Mrs. Oliva Barker for her great care and patience with the secretarial side.

INTRODUCTION

Flowers have always possessed the special magic of bringing life and colour to a room, and 'doing the flowers' has given countless women great satisfaction. As the interest in flowers and foliage and their form has progressed, and the study of growing become more popular, what in my youth was considered to be a social grace has now evolved into a highly organised business, with its own rules, possibilities and limitations. The fashion in arrangements has passed through the early stages of highly stylised work of copies of the paintings of Dutch Masters to elaborate groups constructed geometrically. In the last few years there has been a change in the air, and, with the greater study and better understanding of plant material, we are at the beginning of a new trend—that of simplicity.

The few rules that exist for flower arranging in the Western World have not been abandoned, but now that the old techniques have been mastered, the new approach can be less conventional. The same principles apply to miniature and full size arrangements alike.

The new trend, or 'the artless art' as it was once described to me, bears all the rules in mind, but, because it is spontaneous and free, the underlying technique is not apparent. Nowadays there is far less of 'the tortured daffodil' school of thought, where stems are contorted into unnatural positions, and far more of the natural line is displayed. Today the flowers and foliage are arranged much as they grow, allowing each flower, and each stem, to suggest its own position in the vase by its own form and grace. As we would naturally suppose, this type of arrangement takes far fewer flowers and costs whatever one is prepared to spend. Gone are the days when one's wealth was measured by the fabrics one wore or the type of flower one used when entertaining. Roses, carnations and sweet peas, with the attendant mass of asparagus fern were the criteria of one's social status. We have Constance Spry to thank for this revolution, for with her great foresight and a penchant for de-bunking the ostentatious, these conventions were thrown aside.

Nasturtiums casually arranged in sea-shells for a luncheon table was one of the first non-conformist table decorations created by Constance Spry, and from that time until the present day, the perception and appreciation of form and texture and natural material has progressed beyond all bounds. Cost of material no longer enters into this sphere. Humble flowers, whether small, medium or large, have their own special values, by virtue of their size, density of colour or shape, and their usefulness for the prospective project. This point is well illustrated in plates Nos. 49 and 63: an egg-cup filled with wild flowers and a miniature wooden barrel filled in the most simple way with the seed heads of the dandelion, or 'clocks'. Elaborate sophistication is for the special occasion when a conventional vase is called for, but for everyday, simplicity is the keynote.

Interest in flower arrangement in the past twenty years has spread throughout the British Isles, beginning in Dorset, London, Leicester and Colchester. The influence of the late Constance Spry and her disciples is very much felt here, on the Continent, and to this day throughout the world. Her free style of arrangement befits our older houses with their mellow antique furniture, and from this early influence the Flower Decoration Societies have been formed. Here, at regular meetings, flowers for all occasions are demonstrated—from the very large Church group, to arrangements for side tables, dinner tables and, last but not least, to miniatures.

Miniature flower arrangements nowadays are very much a part of both home life and the competitive show bench. I like arranging these very small groups, but I also enjoy arranging Church groups, and basically the principles are the same. For several years now, in the decorative classes of the Horticultural and Decoration Societies' Shows, miniature arrangements have caused quite a sensation. This interest is still increasing, for any amount of pleasure may be had by displaying wild flowers, alpine flowers, mixed green foliage and fruit in this way, for the side table or mantelpiece, where they take up little space. The containers, as in full size arrangements, can be absolutely anything which will hold water, from thimbles to snuff-boxes and egg-cups to salt-cellars.

Miniature flower arrangement is a great test of patience and ability, as in fact is flower arrangement in general. It is an art and a pastime which can be geared to one's own way of life, according to the amount of time or money, one cares to devote to it. The containers themselves can cost a great deal or only a few pence, likewise the material you choose to use, but, whichever way you decide to follow this pursuit, it can give only unending pleasure and satisfaction.

PREPARATION OF MATERIAL

The preparation of material—cutting and conditioning as it has now come to be called—is very important. I have found on my travels around the British Isles, talking to members of Flower Decoration Societies, Horticultural Societies, hotel managers and girls' schools, that there are many more people interested in flower arrangement who know nothing of this very important subject than those who do.

It is the well-prepared flowers and foliage that are going to last when cut and arranged. It is quite useless to go to great trouble arranging them if they are not going to last well. A withered leaf or drooping flower can ruin the look of an arrangement.

Through long experience we have learnt a great deal about the lasting qualities of plant material under varying conditions. Heat, cold, humidity, currents of air, and even near airlessness, are all vital considerations. Flowers in your own home, picked fresh from the garden, may last well without a great deal of preparation, but I have found it more beneficial for the material for miniature (and large) arrangements alike to have the same basic treatment.

Starting at the very beginning, the time of day that one cuts material from the garden or the hedgerows is important. I find that during the summer months it is far better to cut first thing in the morning or late at night, when it is cool.

Many professional gardeners are trained to cut with a knife, which gives a large area of slanting surface to facilitate the absorption of water. However, I prefer to work with scissors, and I, therefore, have to take a little more care as the cut surface is of necessity smaller. In hot weather it is better to take a bucket of water round the garden with you, and plunge the stems straight into the deep water.

General points which I think are well worth remembering are these:

Soft stemmed material needs only a slanting cut and then an hour or two in deep cold water. Daffodils, narcissi, cowslips, primroses, alstroemeria and lilies give a good example of this type of stem.

Hard stemmed material needs to be split for an inch or two, or hammered to crush the end, so that the sap-bearing vessels are quite free to work. Examples of this type of stem included roses, chrysanthemums, stocks, wallflowers, the stems of flowering shrubs and branches of trees, flowering and otherwise. Remove the lower leaves from stems and the thorns and lower leaves from roses, in fact remove all foliage that will come below the water-line, as it is not only superfluous but it can soon foul the water. Some garden subjects need a little extra assistance for lasting, especially the woody stemmed philadelphus, lilac,

11

(syringa), guelder rose (viburnum): apart from their split or hammered stems, the leaves surrounding the flowers should be removed in order to reduce transpiration and to leave the flower heads free of unnecessary green.

There are several ways of lengthening the life of flowers: by hot water treatment, by boiling, by deep cold water, by iced water, by submersion, by filling hollow stems. Then there is burning, adding sugar, charcoal, or antiseptic to the water, and by using a recent introduction from Holland, a plant food dissolved in water called Chrysal.

Many wild flowers will last as long as cultivated ones if, on reaching home, the stems are re-cut and placed in hot water—110°F or 43°C. The life of bluebells can be prolonged for ten days if they are plunged into hot water for twenty minutes or so, and then arranged in their permanent position. Wood anemones, groundsel and chickweed and many more wild flowers have all benefited from the hot water treatment. In fact the anemones I have used in the shallow dish had suffered very badly on their journey home, but with stems re-cut and plunged into hot water they recovered in a matter of minutes. So quick was their recovery that I could see them moving and very gradually straightening up. Wild daises, with their thread-like stems can also be made to last when treated in this way. Cow parsley and willow herb and many of the taller wild plants must have reached a certain stage of maturity before they can be expected to last.

Some flowers respond well to the boiling of the tips of the stems. With shallow boiling water and foliage and flowers well protected from the steam, the stems should be held in the water for ten seconds, then removed and placed in deep cold water. Many flowers from the herbaceous border, like verbascum, sidalcea, lupins and dahlias, benefit from this treatment.

Deep cold water suits so many cut flowers and foliages that one might say that this is the best treatment; however there are the daffodils and narcissi, large and small, which quite definitely dislike deep water, so their spell in deep water for revival must be brief and they can then be arranged in shallow water.

Iced water can be used when flowers are already in good condition, if their development is to be checked, as in the case of roses to be kept in bud.

Some leaves last better if they are totally submerged in cold water for twelve hours; arum and many ferns fall into this category. Hydrangea flower heads, stephanotis and an orchid: odontoglossum, can be safely left upside-down in water all night. Taken out and gently shaken, they can then dry off and resume their natural beauty. Some flowers prefer to be quite damp, Violets especially, wild or cultivated, may be dipped head first in water and shaken out. They always prefer to be moist about the head and with their stems well down in the water. If these conditions can be maintained their life will be prolonged, which of course is quite understandable when one considers their natural surroundings of cool, damp moss.

Hollow stemmed flowers like delphiniums and lupins benefit from their stems being filled up to the top with water and the cut end plugged with cotton wool.

Sugar dissolved in the water, a dessert-spoonful to half a gallon of water, acts as a stimulant and a food for the flowers.

Iceland, Shirley, Oriental and wild poppies seem to respond better to their stems being burnt. This can be done over a gas flame or with a match.

When the weather is hot, or central heating keeps up a high temperature in the home, a piece of charcoal placed in the bottom of a vase will keep the water sweet, so too will one drop of household disinfectant.

Some flowers prefer to be quite damp, such as violets. Other flowers must be kept quite dry or their petals will become spotted: sweet peas are a good example of this more delicate texture.

Mimosa, hard or soft leafed, and all hard stemmed flowers, last longer if their ends are split, placed in warm water and the flowers sprayed lightly with a fine mist of water, but the important point to remember is to leave mimosa in its near air-tight condition until it is required.

A point which is always raised by those interested in the subject of flower arrangement is; are there any flowers which will not last if mixed together? The answer is; there is no flower or foliage which will not live together in the same arrangement. It has been proved time and time again that if one flower or a certain leaf wilts or dies in a group, then it is for some other reason. Either it is not sufficiently mature, or the stem is blocked, therefore restricting the intake of water, or the room is too hot for its survival, in which case the wilting subject can be removed, re-cut, plunged into the hot water again or in some cases, like the miniature arum leaves, totally submerged in cold water.

Generally speaking, all flowers and foliage react against being placed in a draught; they last better if all the foregoing precautions are taken, remembering of course to top up the containers daily with water.

BASIC PRINCIPLES IN THE ARRANGEMENT OF FLOWERS
Radiation. Proportion. Balance. Harmony and Colour, and terms used in relation to Colour.

My aim in writing this book is to bring flower decoration in miniature into homes where small flowers are admired and appreciated; but, in order to understand the arrangement of them, it is necessary to know the basic principles.

A group of flowers arranged for decoration should look orderly, graceful and, above all, natural, with the harmonious association of flora, containers and surroundings. The transition and linking of material in a group is essential in providing an uninterrupted flow from the centre of interest as the arrangement extends upwards and outwards. This naturally produces the rhythm. Rhythm in itself is yet another essential point, which balances and relates parts of the group, so that the eye is carried through the arrangement with a feeling of motion.

Contrast in shape, form and texture are of no less importance to the miniature flower arrangement. Small, medium and large forms, glaucous and glossy textures and uneven spacing of material all go to make up the variety and contrast and over-all harmony. I think it is generally accepted that a miniature or small flower arrangement, whether 3, 6 or 9 ins. in height, should be a perfect replica of a full-sized arrangement in balance and proportion. Miniature arrangements are considered to be 4 ins. and under in any dimension. The near miniatures between 4 and 9 ins., and any a little larger than this are just known as 'small'.

A flower arrangement is a picture created in living material. The important points which give it character and lift it above the level of the ordinary are suitability to its surroundings, the purpose for which it is designed, and the choice of material. The arrangement, however large or small, must be in keeping with the setting.

The position of your arrangement is all important so too is the lighting. The group should be placed in such a position that it catches the eye and takes advantage of the available lighting conditions, whether daylight or artificial.

Very light arrangements of wild grasses and foliage or catkins look delightful with the daylight coming directly from behind. This, however, is the exception, as most arrangements look their best when lighted from above and to one side, from an angle of 30°.

If, when you come to arrange your flowers, you can do so *in situ*, so much the better. In order to appreciate a really small arrangement, I suggest you place it at eye-level on the mantelshelf, or, for a child, on a low nursery table or window-sill.

Having taken stock of the surrounding colour scheme—the colour of the wood of the furniture, the walls, the carpets, the curtaining and any other predominant colours of lampshades or cushions—then, and then only, is one ready to proceed with the choice of the container. Then consider the arrangement itself, with its colour, line, balance and the contrast of form in the material used. Allow one colour, line or flower to dominate; then all other elements in the arrangement will be subordinate.

I have been asked, many times, to set out the basic principles of flower arrangement. The most important point is *radiation*. Here, in the Western World, the stems of flowers and foliage must radiate from a central point like the rays of the sun. This is achieved by placing the stems into the support in such a way that they point towards a certain place in the container, whether they be tall or short, central or to one side. With practice, this can be accomplished by skilful cutting and placing.

In order to build the shape of a group, however small, it is necessary to place your highest point in position first, and perhaps the next two tallest either side of it, then your widest ones and so, working towards the centre, build up the whole arrangement; by practised cutting a certain shape appears, forming an outline with a broken line. This framework becomes a skeleton on which the body of the arrangement is based. Never should the stems be placed at unnatural angles, nor should they be allowed to cross each other. Although stems crossing unnoticed can be overlooked, it is important to see that they do not show, as the line and finish of the group can so easily be spoilt.

As can be seen in plate No. 56 a silver salt-cellar filled with scillas, daisies, grape hyacinths and grey leaves, all the stems, tiny as they are, have natural curves, and I have arranged them as near as possible to the way in which they were growing.

The shell in plate No. 16 containing erica, daphne, etc., has a slanting aperture which to me always suggests flowing lines. The mother-of-pearl shell in plate No. 46 filled with wild crab-apple blossom, has much the same line about it. Therefore, a soft flowing line from top to bottom, not rising too high above the shell and the lower end resting on the table, seems to me to be the most suitable shape for such a container. The copper mug, the silver cream jug and, in fact, anything with one handle looks well when the material is arranged high on the handle side, with a break in the line flowing down and over to the other side, as though pouring from the lip. The pewter mug in plate No. 32 is a good example of an as-symetrical design. The pussy-willow, which has beautiful natural curves, helps to give movement which would be impossible with stiff stems. The addition of the ivy helps to give it that extra flow which is necessary for such an arrangement. An urn with two handles always suggests to me a more sophisticated arrangement with a central point and the sides equal, curved and flowing.

May I say here and now that the more one practises, the better one becomes; like every other skilled art, it cannot be acquired in days, weeks or months, but years. Read all there is to read, absorb some of the old flower paintings, watch hotel and shop flowers, florists' displays, the horticultural sections of the County Shows, the village shows. Develop the seeing eye in order to assess at a glance the merits of certain material and, in fact, become more and more critical of other people's work and, more important still, your own. In this way, and in this way only, can one hope to improve one's work.

Proportion is next to radiation in importance. Dividing the arrangement, into three equal parts, the container usually occupies one-third and the arrangement two-thirds; this, of course, is an approximate measurement which should be perceived by eye and not with a tape-measure. The arrangements which are measured with the greatest care appear to me to be far too laboured and precise: they are too 'well done' to be natural. Returning to perceiving by eye: I mean that, although the proportions recommended are one-and two-thirds, much depends on the texture and feeling of the container. When wood, terra-cotta and pottery are used they appear to look heavier than a similar sized object in fine porcelain or silver; by virtue of this illusion, the arrangement in the thicker and heavier looking container can be very much taller and wider. In the same way the height can be less than two-thirds when the container is fine, delicate or shallow.

Taking everything into consideration, proportion can be summed up in the following words—the relation in size between material and container, the accessories, and the stands and the space they occupy.

Balance to me is extremely important, and applies, as before, to large groups and miniature arrangements alike. It is extremely difficult to define. Balance of shape may be symmetrical or assymetrical in design. An example of the former is plate No. 71, a tiny Victorian vase, arranged with miniature roses, forget-me-nots and heartsease; it can clearly be seen that the sides are equal in length and the centre point is in the middle of the container. Now, in plate No. 44 it is just as clear that the highest point is also the centre of the arrangement, although this is well to one side of the container. In order to keep this type of arrangement in balance, the opposite side has greater length and the same side as the height has a shorter and more rounded finish.

Only the experienced eye can see balance and shape. It comes with endless work and practice with comparison and correction by experienced teachers.

The framework of any arrangement is usually made up of light-weight material, with natural curves to form the outline, and larger and heavier flowers and leaves to bring weight to the centre of the group. Overcrowding must be avoided, but this comes with experience. The bronze incense burner with cherry blossom, wild sloe and virburnum burkwoodii is a perfect example of under filling; the shape could have been so easily spoilt by over filling, and even where small arrangements are concerned, a space can lighten and enhance the whole group.

Over-arranging, too, must be avoided. With years of teaching experience behind me, I have found that it is the people with the knowledge of growing

16

and the love of all plant material who achieve the best results, who get the correct balance and contrast in form, who acquire the sparseness, which is far more skilled than overcrowding, and the rhythm and movement which is typical of all Constance Spry arrangements.

The texture of the material, the flowers and foliage, wild or cultivated, is closely related to its container. A classic example of a pet hate of mine, whilst on the subject of texture, is marigolds in a cut glass bowl. Put these lovely flowers into a wicker basket, a mahogany tea caddy, or, if you have nothing else, a strawberry chip-basket, and you have the allied textures: cottage garden flowers in a simple-textured and simple-coloured container. It is very important for wild and simple garden flowers to be arranged in containers of simple materials. Wallflowers, polyanthus, primroses, cowslips, daffodils, narcissi, shrub roses all look in perfect harmony in wicker, wood, pottery, terra-cotta, brass, copper or pewter.

Now for flowers with a different texture, such as tulips, roses, gladioli and all others with a smooth shining surface; their beauty is enhanced by harmonious blending with fine china or silver.

I well remember a very large group which I was asked to arrange for a party in a country house many years ago. The hall where it was to stand was decorated in warm yellows with mahogany furniture. A copper preserving pan was offered to me, and for size and colour it was perfect for the job. I was able to choose any material I liked. I chose azalea, a deciduous one in salmon-orange, double orange tulips, single orange Darwin tulips, some Aladdin (a flame lily-flowered tulip with pointed petals), three heads of clivia, two or three Crown Imperials (fritillary), some giant tawny polyanthus, a pineapple, pink-shaded white grapes, apricots and mushrooms. Picture those colours in your mind's eye and I hope you will be able to see a wonderful collection of allied colours in the perfect setting.

The feeling for colour is something, I imagine, one is either born with and develops over the years, or one has not got at all, and so it is not there to develop.

To say that flowers never clash is nonsense, in my opinion, though perhaps if one is insensitive to colour then it could be said to be true. Many people are deeply moved by colour. It is a wonderful subject for endless study and one in which one can continue to learn and experiment with new and exciting materials, and textures smooth and rough. To be colour conscious is to have one's emotions stirred by beautiful harmonies and stimulated by contrasting colours, especially if one is able to create a work of art with the materials available, whether it be in embroidery, on a canvas or in a flower arrangement. So, therefore, balance in colour should certainly be touched on here, as a finished arrangement must be balanced to the eye not only in shape and form but in colour too. If you look at the frontispiece, you will see that, although there is practically every colour available in the arrangement of spring flowers the balance is perfect. The blue muscari are running from one side to the off-side centre and away down to the other side. The purple and mauve run diagonally through the centre, while the cream and yellow in three groups form a triangle within the outer triangular shape. There lies the balance in colour. The balance in shape is there too, with graceful lines giving rhythm and movement. Back to my same example for one more point—that of re-introducing a colour. The cream 'Cheerfulness' narcissi to one side are balanced by the polyanthus on the opposite side and again on the first side. If a line were drawn right through the group from top to bottom, it could be seen that blue is represented in both halves, yellow likewise and pink and red, so giving a perfectly balanced arrangement of mixed colours.

A colour in its full beauty can only be seen to advantage when it is placed with other colours, either in harmony or contrast. Colour is a very personal subject and entirely dictated by one's own taste. I know there are standards in good taste, design and colour which are generally accepted by the majority of people, but there is always the exceptional twist that makes an individual piece, a work of art.

In small and miniature arrangements the colours are just as important in their reduced settings, as are the background and materials. The accessories we have used in our illustrations help to accentuate a certain colour harmony. The green plate behind the simple primroses, the red and gold cup and saucer in combination with the green and black widow iris are examples of this, while the natural linen cloth with the bronze incense burner filled with viburnum and prunus give the all over effect of a near-monochromatic composition.

Background and, of course, foreground colours are most important in setting off one's flowers. In order to make an already advancing group of colours advance still further, a cold receding colour can be used as a background. An example of this is the blue pottery jug and orange berberis set against a blue-grey background in plate No. 38, which, being complimentary in colour, tends to give depth to the picture. As with all warm colours, the illusion is that they advance, whereas the cooler colours appear to recede. Thus, the jug of berberis stands clear away from the background.

Warm colours, like red, yellow and orange, or advancing colours as they are called, really do just that. They come to meet you, while the blues, greys and mauves, the cool colours, recede and tend to be very much quieter. This is, of course, because the creams, yellows, oranges and reds and all the thousands of tints and shades between them light up well in daylight and artificial light alike, while the greys or blues tend to lose their colour in bad daylight or artificial light. However, the really good strong blue of gentians, acaulis, verna and sino-ornata, does shine under strong lighting conditions as you may imagine in No. 43 Gentiana verna in a transparent Venetian glass bowl supported on three tiny feet and ornamented in gold, with grey foliage of wild potentilla and stachys lanata as a finish to the composition of the arrangement.

18

The line of argument of those who say that flowers do not clash is that because the colours harmonise in an herbaceous border they must harmonise in an arrangement. They quite forget the magic effect of the colour green. The impact of a brilliant colour is lessened by the addition of green foliage. A mixed red flower arrangement can be a complete failure with too much green foliage. Remove ninety-nine per cent of the green leaves, and add a few bronze beetroot leaves, atriplex, prunus or sedum maximum atropurpureum, and you will have the perfect sequence in colour from light red to deep bronze-red.

Green is nature's own peculiar way of calming the nerves. Meadows, lawns, trees, the new foliage of herbaceous plants, paeonies, verbascum, the lime greens of many of the hardy euphorbias, grasses in their thousands, hostas; the neatly folded, the corrugated, the glaucous, the lime green bi-colours, the variegated, the grey green of the romneya, the furry grey of the salvias and the stachys, the shiny evergreens, laurel, magnolia, camellia, aucuba and ivy, a million shapes, colours and textures with one thing in common: they are all green. I delight in green flowers, and find them very soothing—Daphne pontica, Daphne laureola, the hellebores, viridis (the one indigenous to this country), corsicus, foetidus, some of the hybrid orientalis, alchemilla mollis, tiarella, to mention but a few. These flowers, used in conjunction with mixed green foliage and seed pods, all carefully arranged, can give not only an interesting effect, but a cool one, where warm colours make up the surrounding colour scheme. Why indeed was the green room of the theatre so called? For that very same reason: the walls were painted a soft green, the natural, restful colour, in contrast to the bright lights of the stage.

In plate No. 55 you can see a mixed green arrangement in miniature. A tiny lidded white box 2 ins. long and ¾ in. high filled with wire netting and water. The contents—wild potentilla, stachys lanata, variegated periwinkle, ivy, larch, and hosta lancifolia undulata, aquilegia, anemone hepatica, cyclamen and hornbeam. (The lipstick helps to give the comparative size.)

Some of the terms more commonly used in relation to colour are given below; by courtesy of the British Colour Council I quote:

1 *Hue* is that attribute or dimension by which one colour is distinguishable from another, one which bears a particular colour name but no qualification as to tone or intensity. That is, a colour may vary according to the character of the colour itself, whether it is a red, a blue or a green, etc.
2 *Tone* is that attribute or dimension by virtue of which a colour is perceived by the normal eye as holding a position in a light-to-dark scale. That is, a colour may vary according to its degree of lightness or darkness. (The terms 'value', 'luminosity' and 'brightness' have also been used for this particular attribute, but for the purpose of referring to colour sensations influenced by surroundings, the word 'tone' is best.)

2—MFAB

3   *Intensity* is that attribute or dimension by which the brilliance of a hue is revealed. An intense colour is one which contains very little grey, that is a relatively pure colour, pure because of its freedom from mixture with any degrading factor. That is, a colour may vary according to the strength of the colour quality, as to whether it is pure or greyed. (This attribute has also been referred to as 'purity', 'saturated colour' and 'chroma' and spoken of as 'that attribute by virtue of which the normal eye perceives in addition to hue the presence or absence of grey').

Besides these three dimensions there are other terms which are loosely used and which should be defined:

Full Hue: a pure colour (intense colour) free from the sensations of any degrading factor.

Chromatic Circle: the spectrum of full hues in which the rate of change between adjacent colours is constant throughout.

Tint: a lighter tone of any colour.

Shade: a darker tone of any colour. (This term is synonymous with 'dark', except that 'dark' is an adjective and 'shade' a noun. 'Shade' has become very widely used as indicating simply a colour, whether it is light of dark, pure or dull. In fact its use has become so customary that it would be practically hopeless to attempt to obtain a general change, and the word 'shade' should be recognised as possessing this secondary but incorrect meaning.)

Radiation, proportion, balance and colour in all its aspects are equally important, but for a student new to flower arranging I would advise: start at the beginning by practising the cutting of stems in order to get the correct length, and placing them in position radiating from a common point. Once one has the shape, then comes the more exciting stage of choosing the different materials, with the background and existing colour scheme in mind. At this stage one should be inspired to use beautiful natural curves and colour harmonies, interesting and unusual flowers and foliage.

Finally, it can be said that a great deal of pleasure is derived from creating original designs, bearing in mind the basic principles of flower arrangement, without slavishly copying the work of others. In time you will find that you are acquiring the feeling for shape and colour which comes with experience.

SUPPORTS FOR ARRANGING FLOWERS: THE BASIC ESSENTIALS

Whatever the size of the flower arrangement, whether it is vast or minute, all the material has to be supported by some means or another. For full sized groups 2-in. wire netting crumpled up and firmly fixed or tied in the container is the first essential. Pinholders placed underneath the netting are extremely useful in giving extra weight and support to heavier material. Oasis and Florapak, the cellular plastic water absorbent blocks, are excellent for arranging, and very good in prolonging the life of the flowers; they too can be used in conjunction with netting or on their own. For very small containers of about 3 ins., I use 2-in. mesh wire netting, and furtherdown the scale to thimble size I make my own netting by twisting and turning silver wire from a reel into the appropriate size. For even smaller containers I have used sand saturated in water, and on occasions sphagnum moss.

However small the container the method of filling follows the same pattern. The support, whatever its nature, is placed in first and it is then filled with water to the brim; by this method all the stems which are at a near horizontal angle will have as much water for their particular needs as those which are upright.

The group of gentians in the Venetian glass bowl was arranged in moss; the mixed green group in the lidded box is also in moss. The pottery jug of muscari and scillas had silver wire netting placed in the neck. The three Venetian glasses arranged together were filled with damp sand and topped up with water. In the group of roses and alpine strawberries, water saturated 'Oasis' was used to fill the cigar-top container.

The reason for using different supports is dictated by the type of stem of flower or leaf. Thread-like stems, if hard, can be placed very successfully in 'Oasis' and the soft stems into sand or moss.

CONTAINERS AND THEIR CONTENTS

The success of an arrangement, as I have said before, is not only judged by the impact that it makes on the eye by its colour or shape, but by its potential lasting properties, and this point we must dwell on now, starting of course with the container. It must be well proportioned, with a wide and generous capacity allowing the material to be arranged unconstricted by a narrow neck.

Once 'wired up' correctly a support may be left in for future use and only removed for cleaning purposes.

Building up a good collection of miniature containers can be a very interesting side line. Some of them are always with us, as in the case of jam dishes and salt-cellars, but the more interesting ones are the bargains from junk shops and the more sophisticated from the sale room or antique shop. Miniature vases designed for flowers in the Victorian and Edwardian era are a great delight and can be bought quite easily. I now have an excellent collection of very small containers in every possible size, shape, colour and texture, some extremely valuable and some quite worthless, but all combining to make a well balanced set. In recent years a collection of delightful Victorian miniature containers has come into my possession, all full of character in their small way.

The lustre of pewter has its special charm, and, whether you prefer it polished or not, the colour is a perfect foil for flowers. I have used it with pussy willow in one arrangement and with snowdrops and Roman hyacinths, merely tossed into a half-gill measure, and the colour, or lack of it, I find very pleasing.

Copper and brass too are excellent colours for the cream, yellow, orange, rust and brown range. In plate No. 26 you may see just such a colour scheme, ranging from the pale yellow of the cowslip to the deep reddy-brown of the horse-tail spikes, arranged in a half-gill copper measure and placed on a piece of un-polished wood it gives just the feeling that was intended: a good colour harmony with simplicity.

Brass has the same useful colour as copper—the green, cream, yellow, orange range, and in plate No. 53 polyanthus and hellebores are grouped together in a very small brass cauldron.

In the same manner, flowers ranging from white to pink to deep rose, to mauve and magenta, will always look right when arranged in a vessel of white or off-white, pale pink, silver, grey tone, or pewter. This, of course, does not mean that other colours cannot be used, but this is a good guide. Pastel shades for containers are always safe to use, providing as they do the background note to an arrangement.

Tertiary colours, grey, bronze, dull reds and celladon green are quite safe to use and will not detract from the flowers, but enhance their beauty in every way. In fact, tertiary colours introduced either in the arrangement or as the colour for the container give a feeling of subtlety which cannot be achieved in an arrangement of primary or secondary colours alone.

Hand in hand with the colour of the container goes the suitability in texture. Simple garden flowers, like wallflowers, polyanthus, marigolds, buttercups and many wild flowers look more charming in the most simple of containers. By this I mean simple shapes and materials: for example, the anemone pulsatilla in plate No. 54 in a wooden bowl, but with a patina that only oiled wood can give. In this same colour range comes polished wood, natural wood and basketwork, tortoiseshell and bronze.

Porcelain, pottery and glass are our next concern, plain and decorated. I am very fortunate in possessing and being able to borrow beautiful little pieces of hand-decorated porcelain, the pattern of which I have been able to copy in real flowers. The 1-in. high Limoges vase with roses on the obverse side and the Rockingham urn with a mixed bunch of flowers are good examples of this. Filled with flowers of the colouring in the decoration they look very charming.

Glass, whether cut, plain, frosted or decorated, is a good medium. I have used my simple pink crackle-glass jam dish with a collection of pink to red flowers, with raspberries, alpine strawberries and blackcurrants. A $\frac{1}{2}$-in. Venetian bowl decorated with gold and filled with gentians, and a more unusual vase of frosted glass with aquilegia shown in relief on the sides, are both illustrated in plates Nos. 43 and 72; these I have been able to match not only in shape but in colour.

Last, but not least, come the valuable patch-boxes, snuff-boxes, toothpick boxes, and all the assortment of tiny things which will hold water; thimbles, tops of detergent bottles, offcuts, driftwood, all in miniature, go to make up a balanced assortment for under-sized arrangements throughout the year.

A model china cup and saucer may be the exact texture and shape for a display of miniature roses. An enamelled snuffbox or patch-box has the advantage of a very decorative lid and holds sufficient water for the needs of the contents. The prices vary for these tiny boxes according to their market value. They may cost anything from £10 to £30 each. My silver swan of 1 in. is quite a treasure, filled with the delightful pink edged daisies from the lawn. One can easily see how much fun can be had from saving and buying and even making some of the containers which go to make up a good collection for miniature flower arrangements.

FLOWERS AND FOLIAGE THROUGHOUT THE YEAR

As we turn into the New Year, leaving December and Christmas behind us, we are able to focus our thoughts once again on the planning of fresh seeds and plants for the garden. The new catalogues arrive and the choice before us is a little bewildering; however, to choose and anticipate enjoyment from something quite new is the best tonic I know for the New Year. My suggestions for flowers and foliage will perhaps help gardeners and lovers of small flowers for use in their miniature arrangements throughout the year.

January can be a very dead month during a hard winter, but given mild spells there are found in the garden many flowers which can be cut and enjoyed indoors; Winter jasmine, Erica carnea, Hammamelis mollis (or witch hazel), aconites, snowdrops, scillas, bergenia, willow, chimonanthus (or wintersweet), Viburnum fragrans, Daphne mezereum and laureola, and early crocuses.

Following on from January into the flowers and foliage under the general heading of spring we have blue and white muscari, auricula and chionodoxa, hellebores, woodland flowers including wood anemones, snowdrops, the sweet violet and oxalis.

Yellow flowers predominate in the spring in the British Isles, and this is the colour that we associate with this season of slowly increasing sunshine. Miniature daffodils, jonquils and narcissi, jasmine, and mimosa from the West country with the added wealth of wild flowers; cowslips, primroses, coltsfoot and celandines, leading on to our commonest but loveliest of wild flowers, the buttercup and dandelion. The little wild Welsh daffodils are most suitable for small arrangements, but, of course, are more difficult to find as their popularity increases. A good effect can be made with a very few flowers arranged in such a way that the individual heads are standing at different levels and in this way each head can be seen clearly, as it takes only a few flowers to produce a deliciously fragrant and woody scent.

For the complimentary green colour to accompany spring flowers, there are the hellebores; orientalis, corsicus, foetidus and viridis, green and white fritillary and auriculas, the fresh green shoots of deciduous trees, larch, catkins, the immature leaves of the hostas, primroses and polyanthus and, where one would use an enormous bergenia leaf in a full sized group, a shortia leaf, which is of much the same texture, can be used in a miniature group. These, with epimedium and miniature ferns, and cyclamen, ivies and grasses, can be invaluable to the arranger. Arisarum proboscideum, the miniature arum species, has the most useful leaves, like small spear heads, with the colour and shape and texture of its full sizes relation the zantedeschia.

24

As we pass almost imperceptibly from spring to summer we become aware of the changes in colours of the seasonal flowers, and the gradual appearance of tiny fruits, alpine strawberries and blackcurrants, and seed heads. The small gentians are gradually going out of season and the later alpines, the saxifrages, aubretias, etc. and miniature roses are coming in. These miniature roses are perfectly formed dwarf versions of the larger shrubs. They are ever blooming, and have all the qualities of hybrid tea and floribunda roses, but are reduced in size. Because of their stature, and wide range of colours they can be a very valuable addition to the small garden. They can be forced in containers for the window-sill, or garden room, or they can be grown with great success in the rock garden, adding a little extra colour right into the late autumn, when frost terminates the season's growth.

The majority of miniature roses come from Rosa chinensis minima, which originally came from China, and as recently as the early nineteenth century there were only six cultivars in circulation. Many new varieties have been raised recently from stocks of: Rosa centifolia minima, Perle de Montserrat and Rosa roulettii, some of the progeny of which are scented. There are hundreds of varieties in cultivation at the present time, and some of the older ones have been renamed in recent years. Many of the professional growers of full size roses now keep a good stock of miniature roses, and there are some nurseries who only specialize in these fascinating dwarf rose bushes, so indispensable for the arrangement of miniature groups.

Turning from roses, miniature iris, Lilliput zinnias, miniature pinks and all the grey and variegated foliages, we come on to autumn with dwarf cyclamen, Gentiana sino-ornata, miniature dahlias and chrysanthemums and the ever intriguing fruits, berries, seed heads and miniature dried material, a wealth of choice in fact, which takes us in full cycle from early spring to late winter for the arrangement of miniature groups.

One of the most interesting developments in floral arrangement in the last twenty years has been the ever increasing appreciation of foliage, now used for decoration with flowers and on its own. Several photographs have been included in our collection of miniature arrangements illustrating this point. This new interest, springing as it does from the love of shapes, colours and textures and, above all, contrast in form, is particularly noticeable in the smaller contemporary gardens of the day, as it was when the parklands were planned and planted out with trees two hundred years ago.

Acquiring interesting foliage does present great problems though to townfolk and flat-dwellers. This can be overcome by some florists who will take orders for bunches of mixed foliage, large and small; or one can become a member of a flower decoration society, attending a monthly meeting and getting to know members with large gardens who will supply one's modest needs at regular intervals.

COLLECTION OF MINIATURE CONTAINERS
Plate No. 1
Left to Right
1. Venetian gold decorated glass bowl.
2. Crystal and ormolu trinket box.
3. Glass salt-cellar.
4. Hand decorated old French perfume bottle.
5. Cut glass salt-cellar.

VICTORIANA

Plate No. 2

Left to Right

1. Miniature Victorian egg-shell porcelain cup and saucer.
2. Pale blue and white bucket of egg-shell porcelain of German origin.
3. Beige-coloured ripe medlar.
4. An egg-shell with bird and nest decoration.
5. Decorated basket of white porcelain.

Plate No. 3
Left to Right
1. Copper snuff-box and lid.
2. Georgian silver salt-cellar.
3. Silver and enamel snuff-box.
4. Silver shell salt-cellar.
5. Silver seal-box.

Plate No. 4

Left to Right

1. A Delft blue and white china clog.
2. Wooden tray and pottery jugs.
3. Pewter measures.
4. Pair of Edwardian shoes of wood.

Plate No. 5
MATERIAL FROM THE WINTER GARDEN   January
Container :   Delft clog. Height 1 in. (25·40 mm.).
Contents :   Chimonanthus praecox, winter sweet.
                Helleborus foetidus.
                Hamamelis mollis, witch-hazel.
                Jasminum nudiflorum, winter jasmine.
                Mahonia bealei.
                Primula, primrose, single blue.
Description : During the first week of January it is possible to find all the
                material arranged in the Delft clog. January can be one of the most
                interesting months of the year to a gardener who specialises in
                winter flowering plants.

30

Plate No. 6
MIDWINTER FLOWERS WITH SHELLS AND CORAL   Winter/January
Container :   Mother-of-pearl shell. Height 1 in. (25·40 mm.).
Contents :   Jasminum nudiflorum, winter jasmine.
                 Garrya elliptica.
                 Hedera canariensis variegata, ivy.
Description : The line of winter jasmine follows the shape of the mother-of-pearl
                 shell.

32

Plate No. 7
PEACH BLOSSOM   March/April
Container :   Old Cantonese enamelled vase. Height 4½ ins. (107·95 mm.).
                Width 1¼ ins.
Contents :   Peach blossom.
Description : Peach blossom is so frequently associated with the Far East that
                this combination of flower and container seems most appropriate.

Plate No. 8
PRUNUS AND AURICULA   Spring/April
Container: Green and white perfume bottle. 3½ ins. (88·90 mm.).
Contents: Prunus.
               Auricula.
Description: Wild plum or sloe cut specially for the shapely branches, in
               association with the purple auriculas, make a very pleasant
               harmony with the blue-green of the perfume bottle, which is of
               French origin, and is over a hundred years old. It is almost certainly
               the work of Jacob Petit, who established a factory at Belleville in the
               neighbourhood of Fontainebleau in the year 1790.

                                                                            37

Plate No. 9
EARLY SPECIE CROCUSES   Winter/January
Container: Egg-shell porcelain vase in the form of a medlar. Made in Germany
                in 1880. Height 1½ ins. (38·10 mm.).
Contents: Crocus chrysanthus, 'Cream beauty'.
                Crocus ancyrensis.
                Eranthis hyemalis, aconite.
                Berberis wilsonae.
                Hedera, ivy.
                Alnus glutinosa, alder.
                Ferula, 'Giant Bronze', fennel.
Description: A replica of the fruit of a medlar serves as a suitable container for
                the specie crocuses.

38

Plate No. 10
SNOWDROPS AND ROMAN HYACINTHS   February

Container :   ½ gill measure. Height 2¼ ins. Width 2 ins. (57·15 × 50·80 mm.).
Mug. Height 7½ ins. Width 5 ins. at the base (190·50 × 127·00 mm.).
Pewter plate in the background. 8¾ ins. diameter (222·25 mm.).

Contents :   Snowdrops.
Roman hyacinths.

Description : The purity of snowdrops and Roman hyacinths, two of our earliest
flowers, can be used with great effect in a room, when set against
the dull lustre of old pewter. The large mug was originally a
trophy won in a four-oared race in 1851 by a team from St. John's
College, Oxford.

40

Stage I   The piece of willow on the far right was inserted first, the hellebore following the same line and thirdly the pussy willow to its left. Then to the far left, insert the longest piece of willow, followed by the hellebore and a shorter sprig of willow, to complete this part of the group.

Stage 2   Here the remaining hellebores have been placed in the shell with the dark red mahonia leaf.

42

Plate No. 11
MID-WINTER ARRANGEMENT FROM THE GARDEN
Helleborus abchasicus, Salix daphnoides, Ericea carnea
Container: Mother-of-pearl shell. Size 7 ins. (177·80 mm.).
Contents: Helleborus abchasicus.
              Salix daphnoides.
              Erica carnea.
              Mahonia aquifolium.
Description: One of the many enchanting hellebores has been used for this
              arrangement in a mother-of-pearl shell. The erica, the willow and
              the mahonia blending with all the natural colours.
              Helleborus abchasicus has a very long flowering period, from
              October to April. They are a deep rose pink, deepening to maroon,
              with, the creamy-green stamens common to most members of
              this diverse family, and the lime green nectaries and mottled
              maroon and green stems. They thrive in a cool position.
              The way in which the shell is filled is most fitting to the angle at
              which it naturally rests, with the aperture slanting and to one side.
              The stems are placed in water saturated 'Oasis'. Used as it has
              been to hold this particular collection of material, it is fascinating to
              see the subtle and varied hues of the shell matching those of the
              flowers and foliage.

Plate No. 12.

THE SMALLEST MINIATURE ARRANGEMENT EVER   Winter

Container: Wine glass. Height $\frac{3}{4}$ in. (19·05 mm.).
Contents: Stellaria media, common chickweed.
               Cyclamen neapolitanum, seedling leaves.
               Erica carnea, heather.
Description: A miniature to end all miniatures.

44

Plate No. 13.

FLOWERING SHRUB AND SPECIE CROCUS   Winter/February–March

Container: Porcelain basket, Coalport. Height 1¼ ins. (31·75 mm.).
Contents: Viburnum fragrans.
                Specie crocus.
Description: Arranged in water saturated 'Oasis' this beautifully scented, pale
                pink deciduous viburnum is the perfect companion to the mauve
                specie crocuses.

46

Plate No. 14
COLLECTION OF LATE WINTER FLOWERS   Winter/February–March
FROM THE GARDEN AND GREENHOUSE

Container :   Japanese bone china teacup, made in 1920. Height 1¼ ins. (31·75 mm.).

Contents :   Prunus triloba.
              Spiraea arguta.
              Hamamelis mollis, witch-hazel.
              Erica carnea, heather.
              Mahonia bealei.
              Helleborus foetidus.
              Cyclamen persicum/cross.
              Galanthus nivalis plenus, double snowdrop.
              Muscari armeniacum, grape hyacinth.
              Echeveria.

Description :   Translucent porcelain teacup, decorated in a bright blue and gold, serves as a container for a mixed collection of flowers from the garden and greenhouse of February/March.

Plate No. 15
PINK AND GREY ARRANGEMENT   Winter/February
Container: Victorian/Edwardian ink well, made of iridescent glass, mounted
               on three feet like captive soap bubbles. Height 2 ins. (50·80 mm.).
Contents: Eucalyptus globulus.
               Erica carnea, 'Springwood pink', heather.
               Cyclamen persicum/cross.
               Saxifraga umbrosa, London Pride.
Description: Fleeting colours of a soap bubble are captured in the grey, the pink,
               the white and green of the simple arrangement. The cyclamen is a
               very new scented hybrid introduced into this country from East
               Germany.

50

Plate No. 16
ERICA CARNEA, ETC.   Spring/March
Container :   A sea shell. Length 3½ ins. Height 2 ins. (88·90 × 50·80 mm.).
Contents :   Erica carnea.
                Bergenia.
                Daphne mezereum.
                Decorative kale.
Description : All the material arranged in the sea shell can be found in the garden
                in early spring. Erica carnea, Daphne mezereum, Bergenia and
                Decorative kale. Two reels of cotton have been included as a
                comparison for size.

Plate No. 17
CROCUSES   Early Spring/February–March
Container :   A blue butter dish of Looe pottery. Diameter 3 ins. Depth ½ in. (76·20
                mm. × 12·20 mm.)
Contents :   Crocuses.
Description : This small bowl of yellow crocuses and wild ivy gives a sense of the
                first indications of spring, and a promise of nature's more colourful
                months to come.

55

Plate No. 18
SNOWDROPS AND SPIRAEA   Winter/January–February
Container: Modern Japanese vase, made in about 1920. Height 1¼ ins. (31·70
              mm.).
Contents: Galanthus nivalis plenus, double snowdrop.
              Spiraea arguta.
Description: Double snowdrops from the garden and forced spiraea from the
              greenhouse make a very happy combination.

Plate No. 19
WHITE, GREY, GREEN AND BLACK   Winter/January–February
Container :   Edwardian silver inkwell. Height 1¼ ins. (31·75 mm.).
Contents :   Erica carnea 'Springwood White', white heather.
              Salix lanata, willow.
              Hebe, 'Veronica'.
              Helleborus viridis.
              Prunus spinosa, blackthorn.
Description : A silver inkwell filled with 'Oasis' and its lid propped open serves
              as a delightful container, arranged with high-key colours of silver,
              white and grey.

58

Plate No. 20

A SYMPHONY IN GREEN AND BLACK   Winter/January–February

Container: Sage green Jasper Ware Wedgwood vase. Height 2 ins. (50·80 mm.).

Contents: Iris tuberosa, or Hermodactylus tuberosa: widow iris.
              Viburnum opulus, guelder rose.
              Salix melanostachys, Black willow catkin.
              Hedera, ivy berries.
              Alnus glutinosus, alder, catkins and cones.

Description: Black and green, the only colours in this group, with forced iris of
              the East Mediterranean and guelder rose, with the other natural
              material from the garden. The willow, an introduction from Japan,
              with the jet black catkins, strikes an interesting note as it is so much
              more uncommon.

60

For your birthday.

Mother —
I have searched for
something "just right"
and I thought you
and your friends might
enjoy this book.

Happy anniversary —

All love from Jean & Jim

Plate No. 21
SHADES OF GREEN AND BLACK   Winter/January–February
Container: A miniature water jug of the 1960's in pewter coloured earthenware
             in the shape of a fish. Height 2¼ ins. (57·15 mm.).
Contents: Garrya elliptica.
             Euonymous radicans variegata.
             Helleborus foetidus.
             Hedera canariensis variegata, ivy.
             Ligustrum vulgare, wild privet.
Description: Arranged in 'Oasis', this collection of shapes, colours and textures
             could be arranged throughout the winter months.

Plate No. 22
LATE WINTER FLOWERS OF DAPHNE AND FORSYTHIA Late Winter/March
Container: Meissen porcelain trinket box with ormulu mounts. Height ¾ in.
              (19·05 mm.).
Contents: Daphne mezereum.
              Forsythia.
              Helleborus foetidus.
              Euonymous radicans variegata.
              Fraxinus excelsior, ash buds.
Description: A light-weight arrangement for the delicate porcelain of the trinket
              box.

Plate No. 23

PEDESTAL ARRANGEMENT   Winter/March

Container :   Porcelain soup tureen, from dolls house dinner service ¼ in. (6·35 mm.). Pedestal height 2¾ ins. (69·85 mm.).

Contents :   Daphne mezereum.
Scilla siberica.
Bergenia cordifolia.
Euonymous radicans variegata.
Prunus spinosa, blackthorn.

Description : This arrangement is reminiscent of a very large group, such as would be used for decorating a church or theatre foyer. The classic lines of the blackthorn forming an interesting shape, setting off the flowers.

66

Plate No. 24

LACHENELIA AND EUCALYPTUS   Winter/March

Container :   White porcelain teapot with gold decoration. Height 1¾ ins. (45·54 mm.).

Contents :   Lachenelia, cape cowslip.
Echeveria.
Eucalyptus.
Cassinia fulvida, shrub.
Hedera canariensis variegata, ivy.

Description : Greenhouse and garden help to supply an arrangement which will last for more than a week.

68

Plate No. 25
MIXED BLUE ARRANGEMENT   Spring/March
Container :   Miniature silver rose bowl. Height 2¾ ins. Width 2 ins. (69·85 × 50·80
                mm.).
Contents :   Muscari,
                Crocus.
                Anemone pulsatilla.
                Scilla.
                Rosemary.
                Artemesia.
                Aquilegia.
                Verbascum brousa.
                Kale.
Description : A mixed blue arrangement containing muscari, mauve crocus,
                Anemone pulsatilla, scilla, and, to act as a foil, leaves of rosemary,
                artemesia, aquilegia, Verbascum brousa, and decorative kale.

70

Plate No. 26
WILD FLOWERS   Spring/April
Container: Copper half-gill measure. Height 2¼ ins. Width 2 ins. (57·15 × 50·80
                mm.).
Contents: Hornbeam catkins.
                Coltsfoot.
                Cowslip.
                Celandine.
                Horse-tail spikes.
Description: The rough wooden foreground helps to give the feeling of rustic
                surroundings for this collection of wild material of mixed yellows
                and browns in the copper measure.

73

Plate No. 27
EUCALYPTUS AND ECHEVERIA   Winter/March
Container :   Porcelain vase from Japan, standing on a black wooden base.
              Made in about 1900 near Tokyo. Height 1¾ ins. (44·45 mm.).
Contents :   Eucalyptus foliage and flower buds.
              Echeveria.
Description : Simplicity in colour and shape is the keynote of this very small
              necked vase.

74

Plate No. 28
PRIMROSES   March
Container :   Brass pot. Height 2 ins. Width 2 ins. (50·80 × 50·80 mm.).
Contents :   Primroses.
Description : The container chosen for the primroses is a small hand wrought
                 pot of unpolished brass. Two plates from a Barnstable pottery
                 breakfast service have been used as a background. The simplest
                 form of arrangement only is necessary for a flower which grows
                 naturally in a mass.

Plate No. 29

IRIS RETICULATA   March

Container: Japanese dish. Length 7½ ins. Width 3¾ ins. (190·50 × 88·90 mm.).

Contents: Iris reticulata.

Description: The container for the iris is a Japanese hors d'oeuvre dish 7½ ins.
long, 3½ ins. wide and 1 in. in height. The iris reticulata, in character
with their natural line, are set simply in the shallow dish. Supported
in a small pinholder disguised by green moss.

Plate No. 30
VIOLETS   Spring/March
Container :   Silver trinket box 3½ ins. × 1¾ ins. × 1¼ ins. (88·90 × 44·45 ×
                31·75 mm.).
Contents :   Violets, 'Princess of Wales'.
Description : A silver trinket box 3½ ins. × 1¾ ins. and 1¼ ins. deep. This
                arrangement of 'Princess of Wales' violets with their own leaves
                and wild ivy has been set against a piece of lace, giving the
                impression of a very feminine dressing-table.

Plate No. 31
IRIS TUBEROSA   Spring/March
Container: China cup and saucer. Height 2¾ ins. (69·85 mm.).
Contents: Iris tuberosa.
               Hosta undulata.
Description: Bone china cup and saucer, with a gold design on a red ground. The
               height of the cup is 2¾ ins. Though good china is often displayed in
               a manner similar to that shown in the picture, it can also be used to
               great advantage for flower arrangements, which in themselves can
               enhance its colour and design. The quiet green of the hosta and
               the green and purple-black of the window iris illustrate this point.

79

Plate No. 32
PUSSY WILLOW. SALIX DAPHNOIDES   Spring/March
Container :   Half-pint pewter drinking mug 3¼ ins. (82·55 mm.).
Contents :   Salix daphnoides.
                Pussy-willow.
Description : The picture shown on the page of the open book was one of the
                 delights of my early childhood. It has remained a lasting memory
                 and was the inspiration of this arrangement of pussy-willow and
                 wild ivy.
                        'I sometimes think the Pussy-Willows grey
                         Are Angel Kittens who have lost their way.'

80

Plate No. 33
A WHITE AND YELLOW HARMONY   Spring/April
Container :   Pottery vase from Gruyère. Height 2¾ ins. Width 2¼ ins. (69·85 ×
              57·15 mm.).
Contents :   Dandelions.
              Scillas.
              Wallflowers.
              Azalea.
              Groundsel.
Description : A simple collection of material—dandelions, scillas or white
              bluebells, yellow wallflowers, azalea and groundsel—typical of the
              spring garden, and with the inclusion of the inevitable weeds.

Plate No. 34
DOUBLE WHITE PRIMROSES AND WHITE VIOLETS   Spring/March

Container: Victorian bucket-shaped vase in pale blue egg-shell china. Height
              1¼ ins. (31·75 mm.).

Contents: Primula vulgaris alba-plena, double white primrose.
              Viola odorata, common white violet.
              Primrose leaf.
              Hedera canariensis.
              Cyclamen neapolitanum leaf.

Description: Double primroses are comparatively rare, there are many colours,
              white, cream, yellow, green, etc. They are very good subjects for
              decoration, and last well when cut and used in a miniature
              container. The words of Sacheverell Sitwell so delightfully describe
              the cultural instructions that I here quote his words, from his most
              interesting book *Old Fashioned Flowers.*
              'The rare primrose requires, not unremitting attention, but those
              acts of forethought shown to an ailing invalid. It is a matter of
              draughts and damp; while the light must not be too strong for its
              eyes, or the sun too hot for its petals. And there are Primroses, as
              well, of unexpectedly strong constitution and with the temperament
              of fresh-air fiends. If their nurse understands them, they will thrive,

82

but, also, certain climates suit them more than others. It is, perhaps the melancholy truth that if sufficiently cared for they will always survive. There could be no greater mistake than to imagine that they are capable of looking after themselves. They may seem to disdain these offers of assistance, but, unless help is always available, they will disappoint at just the moment, it may be, before flowering. We are speaking, of course, of the rare and genuine old Primroses. Many of these have an ancestry of one or two hundred years, so that their weak and flighty health is no matter for surprise.'

83

Plate No. 35

DOUBLE WHITE PRIMROSES AND WHITE VIOLETS   Spring/March

Container :   Blue basket, Victorian era egg-shell china. Height ¾ in. (19·05 mm.).

Contents :   Primula vulgaris alba-plena.
Viola odorata.
Alchemilla mollis leaves.
Alchemilla alpina leaves.
Erythronium dens-canis leaves.

Description :   Three-quarters of an inch is the height of the basket, a typical
example of egg-shell china made in Germany at the end of the
nineteenth century; the signet ring included in the picture helps to
give the comparative size. Double white primroses with their own
buds and leaves, arranged in exactly the same manner as a full
sized basket. White violets as companion, with the silvery foliage of
Alchemilla mollis and Alchemilla alpina, and very small leaves,
patterned in bronze, of the dog-tooth violet, Erythronium dens-canis.

84

Plate No. 36
MIMOSA   Spring/March
Container: A Spanish earthenware water vessel set in front of two Branksome
              ware pottery plates. Height of vessel 2¾ ins. Width 4 ins. (69·85 ×
              101·60 mm.).
Contents: Mimosa.
Description: The choice of container and the setting for this simple arrangement
              of the mimosa with the hard leaf, creates a feeling of warmth and
              southern sunshine, so reminiscent of those countries bordering
              the Mediterranean.

85

Plate No. 37
GREEN FLOWERS   Spring/March–April
Container: Leaden urn. Height 4 ins. (101·60 mm.).
Contents: Flowers: Daphne laureola.
                    Euphorbia characias.
                    Helleborus corsicus, foetidus, orientalis, viridis.
                    Iris tuberosa.
                    Sarcococca ruscifolia.
                Foliage:
                    Arum italicum marmoratum.
                    Hedera canariensis.
                    Hosta undulata.
                    Iris foetidissima variegata.
                    Phalaris arundinaceae picta.
                    Vinca major variegata.
Description: This arrangement was made for the benefit of all those ardent
                growers and lovers of green flowers.
                The outline of the arrangement is formed by the euphorbia, the
                sarcococca, the ivy and Arum italicum. The foliage of differing
                textures, shapes and colours is absorbing in itself, but the flowers
                perhaps even more so. The sweetly scented green and bronze
                black widow iris, Iris tuberosa, on the left top of the group, followed
                by Helleborus corsicus, a clear lime green, then Helleborus
                orientalis, a soft green-white, Helleborus viridis, with the deeper
                green flower, and over to the left Helleborus foetidus, a light lime
                green.
                The supporting foliage is worthy of special mention, as I have made
                full use of variegations of green, white and cream, in order to link
                the many tints and shades of green.

86

Plate No. 38
ORANGE BERBERIS   Summer/May
Container: Blue pottery jug. Height 2½ ins. Width 2½ ins. (63·50 × 63·50 mm.).
Contents: Berberis darwinii.
Description: This arrangement of specially selected pieces of Berberis darwinii
               make a very pleasing shape while following the lines of a jug,
               arranged high on the handle side with flowing lines coming from
               the lip. The background/foreground colour of blue was specially
               chosen as a receding colour, used with the yellow-orange in this
               way the colours of the flowers are forced forward in sharp relief.
               This Berberis darwinii, as the name implies, commemorates
               Charles Darwin, who discovered the shrub in Chile, while on the
               epic voyage in the *Beagle* in 1835. It is a fine shrub, evergreen, not a
               very fast grower. It prefers a well-drained loam and does well in a
               sheltered position.

88

Plate No. 39
GARDEN FLOWERS   Summer/May
Container :   Rose coloured crackle-glass bowl. Height 2 ins. Width 4 ins.
                (50·80 × 101·60 mm.).
Contents :   Prunus foliage.
                Cream broom.
                Berberis.
                Geum.
                Polyanthus, assorted, including 'Jack-in-the-Green', one of the
                very old-fashioned flowers.
Description : A mixture of quite ordinary garden flowers with related colours
                running right through the arrangement. The unusual colour of the
                geum is repeated in the colour of the glass, and, in order to blend all
                the colours of the flowers, bronze prunus foliage is used.

91

Plate No. 40
A WHITE AND CREAM COLLECTION   Early Spring
Container: White Italian porcelain cherub supporting shell. Height 3½ ins.
(88·90 mm.).
Contents: Sprays of wild cherry, white Roman hyacinths, straw coloured
hyacinth 'City of Haarlem', erythronium, white, Lamium
galeobdolon variegatum, Lamium maculatum aureum, yellow,
freesia, white and yellow, fritillaria, white, narcissus 'Cheerfulness',
cream, arum italicum leaves, Ruta graveolens variegata, rue.
Description: Mixed whites, creams and pale yellows are the colours of this
arrangement of flowers cut from the spring garden, with the
addition of glasshouse freesia. The cherubs, facing in two
directions, give it neither a front nor a back, making it especially
useful for a centre position, a sofa table, perhaps.

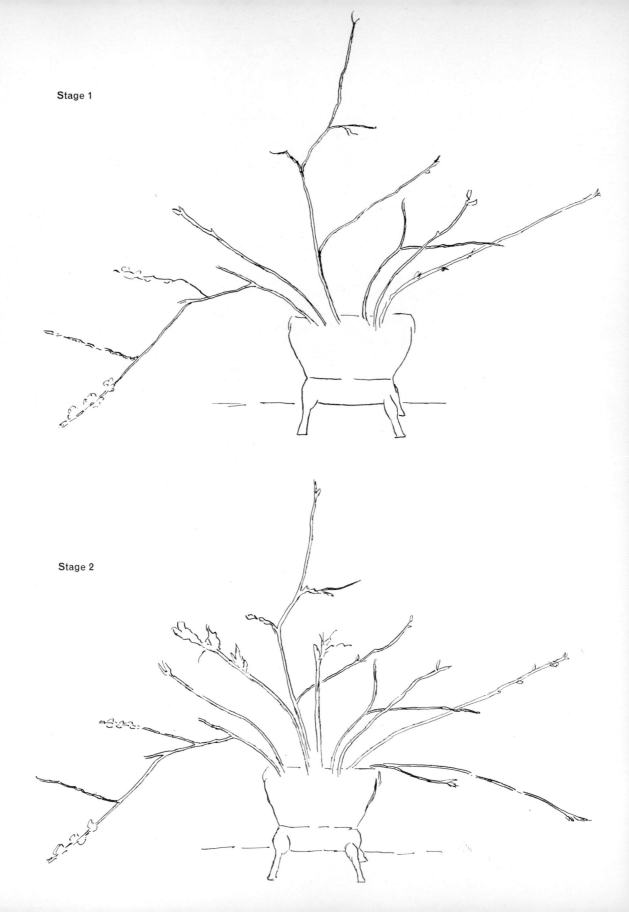

Stage 1

Stage 2

Stage 1   Carefully chosen stems form the outline.

Stage 2   Insert the Viburnum.

Plate No. 41
MONOCHROMATIC COLLECTION   Spring/April
Container : Bronze incense burner with lid. Height 3 ins. (76·20 mm.).
Contents : Wild plum.
              Wild cherry.
              Virburnum burkwoodii.
Description : The burner holds material shaded from cream to bronze, with wild
              plum or sloe, wild cherry and Viburnum burkwoodii. The treatment
              for material such as this is lightness and delicacy, in order to
              appreciate the natural lines.

95

Plate No. 42
WOOD ANEMONES   Spring/April
Container :   Rose coloured crackle-glass dish. Height 2 ins. Diameter 4 ins.
                (50·80 × 101·60 mm.).
Contents :   Wood anemone—Anemone nemorosa.
Description : Wood anemones, following their natural way of growth, are
                arranged in a rose-coloured crackle-glass dish, which reflects the
                delicate colour of the outer petals.

96

Plate No. 43
GENTIANS   Spring/April
Container : Venetian glass bowl with gold engravings. 2 ins. × ¾ in. (50·80 ×
              19·05 mm.).
Contents : Gentiana verna.
Description : Beautiful Gentiana verna arranged entirely on their own, with
               nothing to detract from their simplicity except the soft grey foliage
               of potentilla and stachys.

Plate No. 44
WILD CATKINS   Spring/April

Container : Engraved silver Russian drinking glass and holder. Height $2\frac{3}{4}$ ins.
Width $2\frac{1}{2}$ ins. (69·85 × 63·50 mm.).

Contents : Hornbeam.
Willow catkins.
Wild arum.

Description : In blending various shades of lime green, as found in the hornbeam
and willow catkins, with wild arum leaves, a very restful
arrangement can be made, typical of the coloration of the spring
countryside.

Plate No. 45
MIXED FOLIAGE   Spring/April
Container: Small sea shell 1¼ ins. × 2 ins. (31·75 × 50·80 mm.).
Contents: Fern.
              Potentilla.
              Stachys lanata.
              Oxalis.
              Sedum.
              Epimedium.
              Euonymous radicans.
Description: Mixed foliage of varying shapes, colours and textures from the
              garden and hedgerow, arranged in a very small sea shell.

99

Plate No. 46
CRAB APPLE   Spring/April
Container: Mother-of-pearl shell 3¼ ins. × 5 ins. (82·55 × 127·00 mm.).
Contents: Malus: Crab Apple.
Description: Specially selected pieces of wild crab apple chosen for their shape
               arranged in a flowing line following the aperture of the shell. The
               colour of the petals is repeated in the mother-of-pearl.

100

Plate No. 47
WILD DAISIES   Spring/April
Container: Silver swan. Height 1 in. (25·40 mm.).
Contents: Wild daisies.
Description: Wild daisies from the lawn, used as half-opened buds, so that the
               pink tipped petals could be seen. In order to give a comparison to
               show how very small this arrangement is, a thimble with needles
               and cotton have been included.

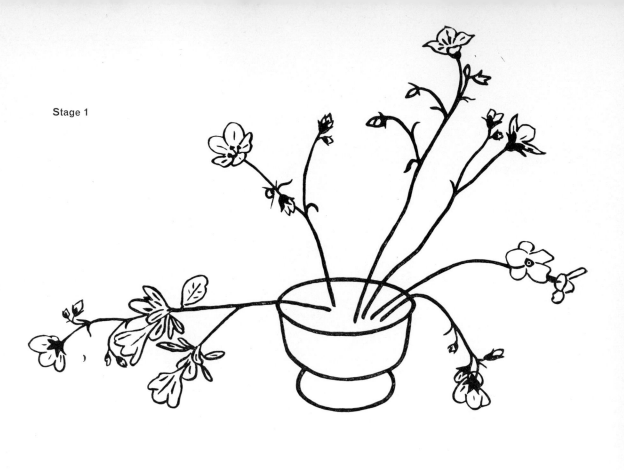

Stage 1   The first six stems are placed in the bowl giving an asymmetrical line.

Stage 2   Further flowers and foilage are added.

Plate No. 48
MIXED ALPINES
Spring/April

Container: Silver bowl 1½ ins. × 2 ins. (38·10 × 50·80 mm.).

Contents: Saxifrage.
                  Azalea.
                  Aubretia.
                  Stachys lanata leaves.

Description: Small alpine flowers in the pink, mauve, magenta range of colours make up the collection in this very small silver bowl.

103

Plate No. 49
WILD FLOWERS IN APRIL   Spring/April
Container :   An egg-cup. Height 2½ ins. (63·50 mm.).
Contents :   Bluebells.
                Buttercups.
                Primroses.
                Lady's smock.
                Violets.
Description : Bluebells, buttercups, primroses, cowslips, lady's smock and
                violets arranged in an egg-cup. The simple material (with the egg
                and spoon included to show the relative size) are suggestive of
                cottage life.

104

Plate No. 50
AN UNUSUAL BUT MUCH-LOVED ARUM SPECIES Late Spring/April–May
Container :   A shallow silver ash-tray, with a baited mousetrap for size. Height
              ¼ in. Width 2½ ins. (6·35 × 63·50 mm.).
Contents :   Arisarum proboscideum, or mouse plant.
Description : The mouse plant Arisarum proboscideum is a delightful and
              unusual plant to grow. Their arrow-head shaped glossy leaves set
              off so well the mice, the weird yet characteristic flower of this arum
              species. The flowers are never visible in the normal way when they
              are growing. A dense collection of leaves is its normal habit of
              growth with only the mouse tails showing through.

105

Stage 1	Beginning at the back of the container, place into the wire netting the two tallest roses and the stem of wild strawberries. Over to the left, in the following order insert the escallonia, honeysuckle and sprig of raspberries. Then to the right of the arrangement put into position the raspberry, the strawberry and the black currant stems.
Stage 2	At this stage the shorter red roses are added, one by one as they run down through the centre of the group. Lastly, to complete this group, all the small pieces which give it its character are added—thus giving the final touches to the shape, the depth and the colour.

Plate No. 51

AN ARRANGEMENT OF SHADED PINK AND RED FLOWERS AND FRUITS IN A CRACKLE-GLASS JAM DISH

Summer

Container: Rose coloured crackle-glass bowl. Height 2 ins. Width 4 ins. (50·80 × 101·60 mm.).

Contents: Miniature red rose 'Baby Crimson'. Honeysuckle. Lychnis. Black-currant (fruit). Wild strawberry (fruit). Geranium. Raspberry (fruit). Escallonia. Aquilegia leaves.

Description: This small arrangement of mixed pink and red flowers was made in a crackle-glass jam dish 2 ins. in height—an excellent shape for such a group with its wide top and tapered stem. The colouring is shaded from the pink of the escallonia to scarlet lychnis and geranium, 'Baby Crimson' rose, raspberries, wild strawberries, honeysuckle, leaves of the aquilegia tinged with purple, and, last of all in the colour range, black-currants. To be appreciated to the full, this small group, like most other miniature flower arrangements, should be placed at eye level.

Plate No. 52
MIXED SUMMER FLOWERS   August/September
Container: Rockingham urn. Height 3¾ ins. (95·25 mm.). Obverse side.
Contents: Liatris.
              Phlox drummondii.
              Roses.
              Honeysuckle.
              Viola.
              Verbascum.
              Gnaphalium or anaphalis nubyana.
              Caryopteris.
              Antirrhinum.
Description: The cream and blue, pink and yellow colours of the china urn are
              all picked up by the living material. A representative bunch of
              flowers from a cottage garden. See plate No. 59 on p. 117.

7—MFAB

Plate No. 53
MIXED YELLOW POLYANTHUS   Spring/April
Container :   Brass cauldron with a handle. Height 2 ins. Width 2¼ ins. (50·80 ×
                 57·15 mm.).
Contents :   Mixed polyanthus.
Description : A group of mixed polyanthus together with a brass container, being
                 warm colours, would bring a feeling of sunshine to an otherwise
                 cold coloured room, as indicated by the light blue foreground.

110

Plate No. 54
ANEMONE PULSATILLA   Spring/April
Container: A brown wooden bowl. 3¾ ins. diameter. Height 1½ ins. (95·25 ×
             30·10 mm.).
Contents: Anemone pulsatilla.
             White anemone pulsatilla.
             Ivy.
             Pussy-willow.
Description: Two shades of mauve Anemone pulsatilla, white Anemone
             pulsatilla, ivy and pussy-willow. Supported by crumpled wire
             netting, arranged in a small wooden bowl.

Plate No. 55
MIXED GREEN FOLIAGES   Spring/April
Container :   Plastic box with lid. Height ¾ in. Width 2 ins. Depth 1 in. (19·05 ×
              50·80 × 25·40 mm.).
Contents :   Larch.
              Hosta undulata.
              Potentilla.
              Stachys lanata.
              Aquilegia.
              Ivy.
              Hepatica triloba.
              Cyclamen neopolitanum.
              Hornbeam.
              Vinca minor variegata.
Description : An arrangement entirely made up of foliage of different colours,
              shapes and textures. Larch, hosta, wild potentilla, Stachys lanata,
              aquilegia, ivy, Hepatica triloba, Cyclamen neapolitanum, hornbeam,
              variegated periwinkle.

112

Plate No. 56
MIXED BLUE FLOWERS   Spring/April

Container :   Silver salt-cellar. Height 1 in. Diameter 1¼ ins. (25·40 × 31·75 mm.).
Contents :   Scillas.
                Forget-me-nots.
                Muscari.
                Wild daisies.
                Potentilla.
                Stachys.
Description : The mixed blue flowers and the silver salt-cellar are blended by the
                use of grey leaves, and the indication of the scale is given by the
                bunch of keys. Scillas, forget-me-nots, muscari, wild daisies,
                arranged with grey foliage, potentilla leaves and Stachys lanata.

113

Plate No. 57
A GOLDEN COLLECTION   Spring/April
Container: Pewter salt-cellar with lion-head feet. Height 1 in. Width 2 in.
              (25·40 × 50·80 mm.).
Contents: Polyanthus.
              Helleborus orientalis.
              Cowslip.
              Foliage of Paeonia mlokosewitschii.
Description: The golden collection of mixed polyanthus, cowslips, Helleborus
              orientalis and the early bronze leaves of the yellow paeony
              (P. mlokosewitschii) arranged in a pewter salt cellar.

114

Plate No. 58

MUSCARI AND FORGET-ME-NOT　　　　　　　　Spring/April

Container :　　Pottery jug. Height 1¼ ins. (31·75 mm.).

Contents :　　Muscari.

　　　　　　　　Forget-me-not.

　　　　　　　　Daisies.

　　　　　　　　Violets.

　　　　　　　　Celandine.

　　　　　　　　Scilla.

Description :　Where full-size wire netting is used in normal arrangements, for this exceptionally small necked container I used a fine gauge silver wire from a reel and crumpled it into a ball. This, firmly wedged in the neck of the jug, served as a support for the fine stems.

Plate No. 59
GARDEN FLOWERS   Summer/August–September
Container: Rockingham urn. Height 3¾ ins. (95·25 mm.). The reverse side.
Contents: More cream and pink colouring and less blue and purple as a
               complement to the reverse side of the Rockingham urn. See Plate
               No. 52. on p. 109.

Plate No. 60
AN ARRANGEMENT OF TERTIARY COLOURS   Late Spring

Container :   Cream alabaster tazza. Height 3½ ins. (88·90 mm.).
Contents :   Approximate height 10 ins. (254·00 mm.).
                Cytisus praecox.
                Edgeworthia papyrifera.
                Hosta albo-marginata 'James Hogg'.
                Euphorbia polychroma.
                Erythronium dens-canis 'Pagoda'.
                Narcissus cyclamineus pale lemon.
                Primula auricula, grey-mauve seedling.
                Daphne retusa.
                Tradescantia tricolor.
Description : Tertiary colours are the main ones dominating this group. The
                alabaster tazza is cream, shading to sand colour, and that is how
                this arrangement came into being. The dull colours of the flowers
                are revolving round the colour of the tazza. The cytisus and the
                edgeworthia, the erythronium and the narcissus are all a dull
                cream to a very light yellow. The Primula auricula, in the same
                tertiary range of colour, is a grey-mauve seedling, and the Daphne
                retusa a very grey-pink.

Plate No. 61

AN ARRANGEMENT OF FLOWERS FOR LATE SPRING

Container: French crystal and Ormolu trinket box. Height 2¼ ins. (57·15 mm.).

Contents: Viola cucculata: White Violet.
Lily-of-the-valley: Convallaria majalis, C. majalis rosea, and C. majalis foliis aurea-variegatus.
Hosta fortunei 'albo-picta'.
Hosta undulata.

Description: Crystal and gilt with a pale blue quilted lining make up the colour of this trinket box. A most fitting container for lily-of-the-valley, both white and pink. The violet, Viola cucculata, is a most rewarding plant to grow, it thrives in half shade, needs little or no attention, and one is rewarded towards the end of May with beautiful long stemmed flowers of perfect proportion and shape, marked in the centre with purple veins surrounded by charming white whiskers.

121

Plate No. 62
CHAENOMELES JAPONICA   Spring/April
Container :   Pottery butter dish in a soft shade of blue. Diameter 3 ins. Depth 1in.
              (76·20 × 25·40 mm.).
Contents :   Chaenomeles japonica.
              Sycamore foliage.
Description : By the use of only a few individual blooms from a shrub of large
              habit, such as Chaenomeles japonica, a touch of colour can be
              introduced in miniature.

122

Plate No. 63
DANDELION CLOCKS   Summer
Container :   Small teak barrel. Height 3 ins. Width 2¾ ins. (76·20 × 69·85 mm.).
Contents :   Dandelion 'clocks'.
Description : Firstly—catch your dandelion clocks! Having selected them carefully,
                a sudden gust of wind can destroy their delicate form. However, let
                us assume that you have passed that delicate operation and are
                now reaching the point of arrangement. You will find that a shot of
                hair lacquer will set them and prevent the ripe seeds on their
                lighter-than-air parachutes from drifting away. There are few
                occasions when such an arrangement is called for in the home,
                however the dandelion seed heads, or 'clocks' as they are called in
                the country, are great favourites with small children, who like to pick
                them, and the number of times it takes to blow away the tiny
                parachute-like seeds indicates the time of day. The hour glass used
                for timing sermons in the nineteenth century suggests yet another
                way of telling the time. The barrel was made from teak out of H.M.S.
                Iron Duke, the Flagship of Admiral Jellicoe at the Battle of Jutland
                in 1916.

Plate No. 64
RED FLOWERS   Summer/August–September
Container :   Limoges vase. Reverse side. Height 2 ins. (50·80 mm.).
Contents :   Phlox drummondii.
            Fuchsia.
            Miniature red rose.
            Carrot leaves.
Description : Red flowers matching the colour of the reverse side of the
            vase, and the gold decoration matched in colour by the carrot
            leaves.

Plate No. 65
GENTIANS   Autumn/October–November
Container :   Georgian silver salt-cellar. Height 1½ ins. Width 2½ ins. (38·10 ×
             63·50 mm.).
Contents :   Gentiana sino-ornata.
             Ceanothus.
             Linaria.
             Forget-me-not.
             Ageratum.
             Artemesia.
             Asplenium viride.
Description :   A combination of blues, mauves and purples go to make up this
             arrangement in a silver container.

127

Plate No. 66
BLUE AND WHITE FOR COOL SIMPLICITY   Summer
Container: Royal Worcester cream jug. Height 2¾ ins. (69·85 mm.).
Contents: Matricaria recutita: Wild Daisies.
Description: Arrangements of mixed flowers are always interesting and
               exhilarating, but now and again it is not only restful but quite
               absorbing to have a group of one flower only. The wild field daisies
               arranged in the Royal Worcester jug, with the aid of wire netting,
               give the feeling of calm, with the chance to appreciate the beauty of
               each individual flower.

128

Plate No. 67

BLENDING BLUE FLOWERS   Late Spring/May

Container :   Silver cream jug. Height 1½ ins. Width 3½ ins. (38·10 × 88·90 mm.).

Contents :   Bluebells.
                Periwinkle.
                Viola.

Description : In the silver cream jug I have chosen as a complement in shape only
                two other flowers of the same colour, periwinkle—Vinca minor—and
                viola. The arrangement follows the lines of the jug, being higher on
                the handle side and flowing from the lip. The bluebells last so much
                better when given a preliminary drink of hot water before they are
                arranged.

Plate No. 68
LILY-OF-THE-VALLEY   Late Spring
Container :   A silver bowl. Height 1½ ins. (38·10 mm.).
Contents :   Lily-of-the-valley.
            Hosta undulata.
Description : Lily-of-the-valley arranged entirely on its own. The texture, the
            shape of the flowers, the architectural qualities of the stems,
            however small, possess something which is quite unique in the
            flower world, and lend themselves so well to arrangement on their
            own. Lily-of-the-valley foliage and very young Hosta undulata
            leaves are used for finishing the arrangement.

130

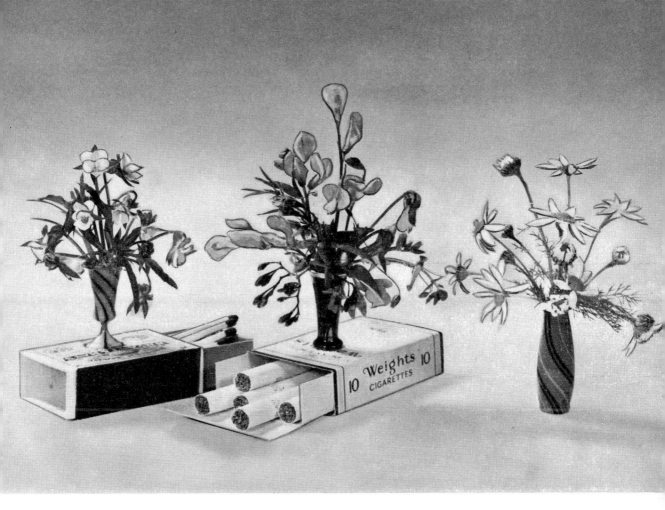

Plate No. 69
WILD FLOWERS   Summer
Containers: Three Venetian glass vases. Height 1 in. (25·40 mm.).
Contents: From left, No. 1 (standing on matchbox) wild heartsease, viola.
               No. 2 (standing on packet of cigarettes) wild heartsease, yellow
               vetch, scarlet pimpernel and woody nightshade.
               No. 3 (standing on plain base) wild daisies, Matricaria recutita.
Description: In each case with these very small groups, damp sand was used as
               a support for the flower stems, and, small as they are, as every stem
               has been individually placed in the container, the value of each
               flower head can be appreciated.

131

Stage 1   The first nine stems placed in postion cutting them to different lengths to form the shape of the outline.

Stage 2   The shorter and slightly fuller roses were added to the arrangement for stage 2—running obliquely through the centre for depth and weight.

132

Plate No. 70

A BOWL OF MINIATURE ROSES   Summer

Container: Blue pottery butter dish. Height ½ in. (12·70 mm.) from Looe, Cornwall.

Contents: Miniature yellow rose, 'Josephine Wheatcroft'.

Helianthemum. Rock rose.

Potentilla effusa.

Potentilla anserina.

Honeysuckle.

Erica.

Cotyledon.

Asplenium: Maidenhair fern.

Description: This very small arrangement of yellow roses 'Josephine Wheatcroft', potentilla and honeysuckle in a blue pottery butter dish from Cornwall is less than 4 ins. high. It is typical of what can be achieved with very simple materials, using fairly opened roses instead of tight buds.

133

Plate No. 71
ROSES, FORGET-ME-NOTS AND HEARTSEASE   Summer
Container :   Victorian egg-shell china vase. Height 1¼ ins. (31·75 mm.).
Contents :   Myosotis: Forget-me-nots.
           Viola tricolor: Heartsease.
           Polygonum persicaria.
           Gnaphalium sylvaticum.
           Rose, 'Cécile Brunner'.
Description : A simple and light arrangement in a Victorian miniature vase. A
           signet ring is included to indicate the size.

134

Plate No. 72
A GALLÉ VASE AND AQUILEGIA   Summer

Container :   Glass vase by Gallé. Height 3¾ ins. Width 2¾ ins. (95·25 ×
                69·85 mm.).
Contents :   Aquilegia.
Description : An interesting combination of a decorated glass, a signed piece by
                Gallé, made in about 1900 in Nancy with the exact replica of the
                decoration in the arrangement. The medium spurred aquilegia, in
                much the same colour as the glass, cream and pink-rust.

Plate No. 73
ROSES   Summer/August–September
Container : Limoges vase. Height 2 ins. (50·80 mm.).
Contents : Three miniature roses, 'Baby Crimson'. 'Cécile Brunner' and
              'Rosa roulettii'.
Description : The vase, a deep red and gold, with the hand-painted rose on the
                obverse side. A simple collection of miniature flowers, picking up
                the colouring of the china.

137

Plate No. 74
GENTIANS   Autumn/October–November
Container: Silver mustard-pot. Height 1½ ins. (38·10 mm.).
Contents: Gentiana sino-ornata.
                      Erica carnea.
                      Stachys lanata.
Description: Following the line of a lidded container, the gentians are arranged
                      highest on the side of the lid, flowing over to the opposite side,
                      where there is the extra length, ending with a beautifully shaped
                      bud.

138

Plate No. 75
HAND DECORATED LIMOGES VASE WITH MINIATURE PINK ROSES
Summer/July

Container :   Height 2 ins. (50·80 mm.).
Contents :   Roses.
Description : Just a handful of pink roses placed in the hand painted miniature
vase. Maroon and gold are the basic colours of this typical piece of
Limoges china. On the obverse side can be quite clearly seen the
hand painted decoration of a pink rose.

139

Plate No. 76
A SIDE TABLE ARRANGEMENT WITH CONTEMPORARY ITALIAN
POTTERY CHERUB AND ROSES

Container: White Italian pottery shell, supported by a cherub. Height 3 ins.
(76·20 mm.).

Contents: Roses: 'Cécile Brunner', 'Josephine Wheatcroft', 'The Fairy',
'Jenny Wren'.
Astrantia maxima.
Astrantia biebersteinii.
Origanum: Golden marjoram.
Lewisia.
Atriplex halimus.
Macleaya cordata.
Romneya coulteri.
Hypericum olympicum.
Lobelia.
Geranium, maroon and lime green.

Description: Cherubs, shells and miniature roses all seem to blend together in
the most delightful way. The Italian figure pictured here in white
pottery is one of the many contemporary designs now imported.
The overall colour scheme of the material filling the container is
pastel pink, blue and yellow with glaucous foliage.

141

Plate No. 77
MIXED FOLIAGE   Summer/July
Container: Silver salt-cellar. Hight ½ in. Width 1½ ins. (12·70 × 38·10 mm.).
Contents: Sedum sieboldianum.   Geranium.
               Sedum reflexum. 'Chamelon'.   Hypericum: olympicum.
               Sedum spathulifolium.
               Origanum. Golden marjoram.   Saxifrage.
               Bocconia macleaya.   Tellima.
               Linaria.   Fern.
Description: A most rewarding arrangement to do in varying shades and tints of
               green, ranging from yellow green, grey, clear green to bronze,
               supported in this case by 'Oasis' saturated in water.

142

Plate No. 78

"BABY CRIMSON ROSES" AND ALPINE STRAWBERRIES   Summer/July

Container :   Cigar case top. Height ¼ in. Width ½ in. (6·35 × 12·70 mm.).
                Wooden tray. Width 2 ins. (50·80 mm.).

Contents :   'Baby Crimson'.
                Alpine strawberry.
                Macleaya bocconia.
                Thalictrum.
                Hebe or veronica.
                Acaena microphylla.

Description : One of the smallest arrangements ever, an asymmetrical design
                incorporating flowers and fruit supported by damp 'Oasis' in a
                metal cigar holder top.

143

Plate No. 79
COBAEA SCANDENS ALBA   August/September
Container :   Dark green hand thrown pottery vase. Height 5 ins. Diameter 3 ins.
               (127·00 × 76·20 mm.).
Contents :   Cobaea scandens alba.   Clematis tangutica seedheads.
               Hedera canariensis.   Hedera helix.
Description : A symphony of greens.

144

Plate No. 80
CYCLAMEN NEAPOLITANUM AND ROSES   Autumn/October–November

Container :   Pewter salt-cellar. Height ¾ in. (19·05 mm.).

Contents :   Cyclamen neapolitanum.
Rose, 'Josephine Wheatcroft'.
Erica carnea.
Ivy hedera helix: Buttercup.
Hedera helix: 'Chicago' Variegata.

Description :   White and pale yellow are the colours of the flowers in this miniature
group. The ivy and the new flower buds of the erica provide the
matching lime yellow foliage. The fascinating corkscrew stems of
the mature flower and seed head of the cyclamen can be seen
alongside its own beautifully marbled leaf.

145

Plate No. 81
HONEYSUCKLE AND ROSES   August–September
Container :   Belleek shell. Height 3 ins. (76·20 mm.).
Contents :   Honeysuckle.
                 Rose, 'La France'.
                 Rose, 'Cécile Brunner'.
                 Phytolacca americana.
                 Astrantia carniolica major.
                 Cobaea scandens alba.
Description :   The artless art describes this arrangement, a casual treatment of a
                 simple collection of material, soft shades of pink, yellow and green
                 with a delicious scent that only those who have ever grown 'La
                 France', a very old rose, will know.
                 Arranged in an Irish china shell, 3 ins. in height, and supported by
                 2-in. mesh wire netting, are stems of honeysuckle forming the
                 outline of the arrangement. It can be seen quite clearly that a point
                 to a group of flowers can be achieved by a rounded head and not
                 the inevitable spiked inflorescence. The three stems of honeysuckle
                 at the top form the shape of a triangle—however vague this shape
                 may be, the pale green of the phytolacca flowers carry the shape
                 down to the left hand side. Three fully opened flowers of 'La
                 France', a lovely shaped and many petalled rose of soft pink, form
                 another triangle within the larger one, bringing the weight to the
                 centre of the group. Over to the right is a rare colour in a mature
                 flower, that of the Cobaea scandens alba, an ethereal shade of the
                 palest green. Balancing this flower on the opposite side of the group
                 is the soft green calyx of a cobaea and the grey-green of the astrantia.
                 The small roses, also pale pink, are the miniature heads of the
                 polyantha rose 'Cécile Brunner'. A good bush of this rose grown in
                 sunny a position can rise up to six feet or more and be completely
                 covered in hundreds of these perfect miniature roses.
                 This collection of material can be picked from the garden in July,
                 August and September. The roses, the cobaea and the astrantia
                 have a good long season, while the honeysuckle, which normally
                 blooms once in early summer, can be persuaded to repeat the
                 process if it is pruned immediately after flowering. Continually
                 removing the dead heads throughout the summer ensures a
                 succession of honeysuckle deep into the autumn.

146

Plate No. 82
GENTIANS AND ROSES   Autumn/October–November
Container :   Georgian silver salt-cellar. Height 1¼ ins. Width 2½ ins. (31·75 ×
                63·50 mm.).
Contents :   Gentiana sino-ornata.
                Roses.
                Potentilla anserina.
Description : Shining deep blue trumpets of the gentian, with pale pink scented
                rose buds of 'Cécile Brunner' are set off by the silver of the salt-
                cellar and the grey potentilla leaves.

148

Plate No. 83
FLOWERLESS GROUP   Winter/December–January

Container :   A pair of carved wooden shoes. Height ½ in. 3 ins. long. (12·70
             × 76·20 mm.).

Contents :   Geranium quercifolium.
             Geranium, golden 'Harry Hieover'.
             Geranium crispum.
             Ferula 'Giant Bronze', fennel.
             Viburnum tinus 'Lady Eve Price', laurustinus.
             Helleborus foetidus.
             Saxifraga umbrosa, 'London Pride'.
             Sedum.
             Moss.

Description : Greenhouse and garden combine together to supply unusual
             material for the tiny shoes.

149

Plate No. 84
MUTED SHADES OF AUTUMN   November
Container :   Wrought-iron container and smoke-grey mirror base. Height 5 ins.
               (127·00 mm.).
Contents :   Salvia horminum, 'Blue Bird'.
               Salvia horminum, 'Colour Blend'.
               Assorted annual grasses.
               Polygonum affine.
               Bougainvillea.
               Schizostylis.
               Vitis vinifera purpurea.
               Rose floribunda, 'Gletcher'.
               Cobaea scandens.
               Mentha rotundifolia variegata.
               Clematis tangutica seedheads.
               Meconopsis regia.
               Sedum maximum atropurpureum.
Description : All the material in this wrought-iron and glass container comes
               from the open garden in November. The only exception in this
               collection is the glasshouse grown bougainvillea. The colouring of
               all the material is predominantly grey, using it as a foil to the
               smoked mirror glass base of the container. Grey-pinks, grey-
               mauves, grey-greens, all these colours are here with the addition of
               highlights of clear pink of the schizostylis, the soft yellow of the
               mint, to the deep undercurrent of bronze of the vine and sedum.

                                                                        151

Plate No. 85
ROSE HIPS, ALDER CONES AND IVY FOR A MID-WINTER GROUP

Mid-winter/November–December

Container :   A Chinese vessel in hand-beaten copper. Height 1¾ ins. (44·45 mm.).
Contents :   Rosa canina: Wild Rose seed heads.
                Alnus glutinosus, alder.
                Hedera, ivy.
Description : A perfect blend in colour and texture, the lustrous rose hips, so
                typical of our English countryside in winter, arranged with alder
                catkins and ivy trails in a hand-beaten copper vessel.

153

Plate No. 86
TINY TWIGS AND CONES FROM THE WINTER GARDEN Winter/December
Container :   A contemporary Italian earthenware horse. Height 1¾ ins. (31·75
                 mm.).
Contents :   Alnus glutinosa, alder.
                 Berberis wilsonae.
                 Cornus alba (red), dogwood.
                 Cornus stolonifera flaviramea (yellow).
                 Hedera canariesnis variegata, ivy.
                 Sedum.
                 Syringa seedheads (Lilac).
Description : In the depths of winter in the British Isles there is always something
                 to be found in the garden or country-side, such as the twigs, cones
                 and foliage arranged in the earthenware horse.

155

Plate No. 87
CHRISTMAS DINNER TABLE GROUP—CHRISTMAS ROSES, HOLLY AND
WILLOW
Container :   Shallow dish, width 4 ins. (101·60 mm.).
Contents :   Helleborus niger: Christmas Rose.
            Ilex: Holly.
            Salix daphnoides: Pussy Willow.
Description : White, cream and silver are the predominant colours of this
            Christmas table centre. Ivory candles, lace tablecloth and holly,
            silver catkins and candlesticks, pure white hellebores and lumps of
            rough crystal combine to make a high-key arrangement for the
            sophisticated Christmas dinner table.

156

INDEX

158

Helleborus foetidus, 19, 24, 30, 48, 62, 64, 86, 149
Helleborus niger (Christmas rose), 156
Helleborus orientalis, 19, 24, 86, 114
Helleborus viridis, 19, 24, 58, 86
Hepatica triloba (anemone hepatica), 19, 112
Hermodactylus tuberosa (iris tuberosa—widow iris), 18, 60, 79, 86
Holly (ilex), 156
Honeysuckle (lonicera), 106, 109, 133, 146
Hornbeam (carpinus), 19, 73, 98, 112
Horsetail spikes (equisetum), 22, 73
Hosta (plantain lily), 19, 24, 79, 86, 112, 119, 121, 130
Hosta albo—marginata, 119
Hosta fortunei, 121
Hosta undulata, 79, 86, 112, 121, 130
Hyacinth, "City of Haarlem", 92
Hyacinth, Roman, 22, 41, 92
Hydrangea, 12
Hypericum olympicum (St. John's wort), 141, 142

I

Ilex (holly), 156
Iris, 18, 25, 60, 77, 79, 86
Iris foetidissima variegata, 86
Iris—miniature, 25
Iris reticulata, 77
Iris tuberosa (widow iris), 18, 60, 79, 86
Ivy (hedera), 15, 19, 24, 32, 38, 55, 60, 62, 68, 78, 80, 82, 86, 111, 112, 144, 145, 153, 155
Ivy (hedera helix—"Buttercup"), 144, 145
Ivy (hedera canariensis), 32, 62, 68, 82, 86, 144, 155

Ivy (hedera helix—"Chicago"), 145

J

Jasmine, winter (jasminum nudiflorum), 24, 30, 32
Jasminum nudiflorum (winter jasmine), 24, 30, 32

K

Kale—decorative, 52, 70
Kaffir lily (schizostylis), 151

L

Lachenalia (cape cowslip), 68
Lady's smock (cardamine pratensis), 104
Lambs lugs (stacys lanata), 18, 19, 99, 103, 112, 113, 138
Lamium (dead-nettle family), 92
Lamium galeobdolon variegatum, 92
Lamium maculatum aureum, 92
Larch (larix decidua), 19, 24, 112
Larix decidua (larch), 19, 24, 112
Laurel, 19
Laurustinus (viburnum tinus), 149
Lenten rose (helleborus orientalis), 114
Lewisia, 141
Liatris, 109
Ligustrum vulgare (wild privet), 62
Lilac (syringa), 11, 155
Lilies, 11
Lily-of-the-valley (convallaria), 121, 130
Linaria (toadflax), 127, 142
Lobelia, 141
London pride (saxifraga umbrosa), 50, 149, 155
Lonicera (honeysuckle), 106, 109, 133, 146
Lords and ladies (wild arum), 98

Primroses (primula), 17, 24, 30, 76, 82, 84, 104

Primula, 2, 11, 17, 18, 22, 23, 24, 30, 73, 76, 82, 84, 91, 104, 110, 114, 119

Primula (auricula), 2, 24, 119

Primula (cowslip), 11, 17, 22, 24, 73, 104, 114

Primula (polyanthus), 2, 17, 18, 22, 23, 91, 110, 114

Primula (primrose), 11, 17, 24, 30, 76, 82, 84, 104

Primula vulgaris—alba plena, 82, 84

Privet—wild (ligustrum vulgare), 62

Prunus, 16, 18, 19, 34, 37, 48, 58, 66, 91, 95

Prunus—bronze foliage, 19, 91

Prunus—cherry, 16, 18, 19, 95

Prunus—peach, 34

Prunus—plum, 37, 95

Prunus spinosa (blackthorn—wild sloe), 16, 18, 58, 66

Prunus triloba, 48

Pussy willow (salix—wild), 15, 22, 23, 80, 98

Q

Quince (chaenomeles japonica), 2, 122

R

Ranunculus (buttercup), 23, 24, 104

Ranunculus ficaria (lesser celandine), 24, 73, 115

Raspberry fruit (rubus idaeus), 23, 106

Rock rose (helianthemum), 133

Romneya coulteri (Californian tree poppy), 19, 141

Rosa canina (dog rose), 153

Rosa centifolia minima, 25

Rosa chinensis minima, 25

Rosa rouletti, 25, 124

Roses, 9, 11, 12, 16, 17, 21, 23, 25, 106, 109, 124, 133, 134, 139, 141, 143, 145, 146, 148, 151, 153

Rose—"Baby Crimson", 106, 124, 143

Rose—"Cecile Brunner", 109, 124, 134, 141, 146, 148

Rose—"Jenny Wren", 141

Rose—"Josephine Wheatcroft", 133, 141, 145

Rose—"La France", 146

Rose—"Perle de Montserrat", 25

Rose—"The Fairy", 141

Rose—floribunda—"Gletcher", 151

Rose—miniature, 23, 25, 106, 124, 133, 141, 145

Rose—shrub, 17

Rosemary (rosmarinus), 2, 70

Rubus idaeus (raspberry), 23, 106

Rue (ruta graveolens variegata), 92

Ruta graveolens variegata (rue), 92

S

Salix, 43, 58, 60, 80, 98, 111, 156

Salix daphnoides (willow), 43, 80, 156

Salix lanata (willow), 58, 80, 111

Salix melanostachys (willow), 60

Salix—wild (pussy willow), 15, 22, 23, 80, 98

Salvia, 19, 151

Salvia horminum, "Blue Bird", 151

Salvia horminum, "Colour Blend", 151

Sarcococca ruscifolia, 86

Saxifraga umbrosa (London pride), 25, 50, 149

Scarlet pimpernel (anagallis tenella), 131

Schizostylis (Kaffir lily), 151

Scilla, 15, 21, 24, 66, 70, 81, 104, 113, 115, 129

Scilla (bluebells—blue), 12, 129